SPEAK WITH CONFIDENCE

SPEAK WITH CONFIDENCE

A Practical Guide to a Better Voice

Meribeth Bunch

KOGAN
PAGE

First published in Great Britain in 1987 by Pippa Rann Publications,
entitled *The Voice Book*. This revised edition published in 1989 by
Kogan Page Limited, 120 Pentonville Road,
London N1 9JN.

British Library Cataloguing in Publication Data

Bunch, Meribeth
    Speak with confidence: a practical guide to
    a better voice. – 2nd ed.
    1. Public speaking. Manuals
    I. Title   II. Bunch, Meribeth. Voice Book
    808.5'1

    ISBN 1-85091-823-6
    ISBN 1-85091-824-4 Pbk

Typeset by DP Photosetting, Aylesbury, Bucks
Printed and bound in Great Britain by
Biddles Limited, Guildford

Contents

Preface

Is your voice saying what you mean? Can you make yourself heard in a busy, noisy meeting? Do you wish your voice had more power? Does your voice feel strained after you've been talking to a large group of people? Are you comfortable and confident when you are attending an important meeting, briefing members of your staff, or making presentations to the board or sales force?

How you present yourself, whether to one person or to a group, is important. What others experience first is either your voice or your image. While this book is particularly addressed to your voice, you will find that voice and image go together. Therefore image is also very much part of this book.

If you follow the guidelines and exercises, you can improve your voice and enhance your presence. Most chapters contain directives for self-observation and corrective exercises for improving posture, breathing, the quality of your voice and articulation. The exercises are designed to relate to your daily activities and fit into a busy day. There are even suggestions as to how to do two things at once.

Your voice can be refined by a good teacher. However, with the aid of a tape recorder, a mirror and sometimes a friend, you can make many improvements by yourself.

Most people assume that their voices can never be changed. ('That's just my voice. I was born with it.') The voice is not some mysterious entity that functions with a mind of its own. It is made of muscle and cartilage, it can have problems, and it can be adjusted and improved as can many other parts of the body. You can improve the sound of your voice if you wish to make the effort and are willing to sound different to yourself for a while.

It is important for you to realise that your voice as heard inside yourself is not like a recording of it. The recording is indicative of what others hear in your voice. What you hear inside can be very misleading to you and can keep you from making the improvements you need. To make such improvements you must be willing to let your 'inside' voice seem strange and unfamiliar to you for a while.

This book is designed to help you improve your vocal communication and shows you how best to spend your time in acquiring skills basic to sound that is easily and freely produced.

The guidelines and exercises are especially useful for lay speakers, people in business, teachers, actors and students of voice. They are also of value to speech and voice therapists as a guide for correcting speech and voice problems.

The sound of the human voice is a very special joy and it is important in this age of stress and tension that the delightful qualities of your voice are not lost.

Meribeth Bunch
London
November 1988

Introduction

Where have all the warm and charming voices gone?

Have they been lost in the din of ...

Environmental noise at home and work
Traffic noise – overhead and below
Personal radios and tape recorders
Loud TVs and stereos
Your own personal tensions?

Think about the following questions:

- What are your own personal tensions and stress doing to your communication?
- Are you raising your voice to be heard above the background noise?
- Have you ever returned home hoarse after a day of talking on the phone or to customers, a sales meeting, giving a speech or teaching?
- Are you a bundle of nerves when asked to speak casually or formally?
- Do you like your voice as you hear it on a tape recording?
- Does your voice convey your intent?
- Are you truly communicating something of yourself or somehow getting in your own way?
- Is the quality of your voice giving a meaning you do not intend to the words you are saying? (Sometimes we do not know when this is happening.) Tape a conversation with a colleague or friend. Listen to it later as though you were listening to someone other than yourself.
- Is your voice pleasing?

Has it occurred to you that if any of the answers to the above were 'No', you can change what you do not like?

If you think that a voice is a voice and cannot be changed, allow yourself some new thoughts about the matter.

Even though your voice is unique, it can be altered. Such improvements will not lead to the loss of your own special qualities. In fact, what is special about you may become much more apparent.

The chapters that follow include simple suggestions for improving your voice.

1. Always Begin With Posture

Your voice is an instrument.
All instruments must be put together properly to be tuned and
to function efficiently.
Can you imagine playing a bent flute or warped cello?

The body forms and houses the voice and therefore must be in an
alignment which allows you to present your best possible sound
and image.

Make some observations during your daily routine.

- Look at those around you.
- Look at yourself.
- Do the people you see appear at ease and graceful?
- Could you stand or sit more gracefully or are you like a sack of
  potatoes?
- Imagine what kind of voices might come out of the shapes you
  see.

Experiment for a moment with your voice as you move your
body into different positions.

1. Choose a phrase to repeat throughout the exercise. It can be
   something simple like 'What a beautiful day' or 'I love to go to
   work'.

   What happens when you repeat the phrase and
   (a) tuck your chin into your chest
   (b) lift your chin towards the ceiling
   (c) push your chin and head forward
   (d) change the angle of your head in various ways?

The sound changes.

Why? Because you are interfering with various parts of your vocal instrument.

2. While repeating your phrase move your body from a slouch to a taller, straighter, but not a rigid position.

3. Once more repeat your phrase. This time do it while
   (a) caving in your chest
   (b) rigidly pulling your shoulders backwards.

4. For the last time, while continuing your phrase,
   (a) make your whole body tense and rigid
   (b) release the tension.

With all these exercises there will be changes in your sound. If you cannot hear the differences yourself, check your tape recording or ask a friend to listen. As tension is released and the muscles are allowed to function efficiently the sound will improve.

The vocal instrument

Most other instruments have solid, rigid structures which do not yield and therefore have stable tonal qualities. This is not true of the body. It is a fascinating instrument because many of its parts are used for other bodily needs such as breathing (lungs), protecting the lungs (larynx) and eating (mouth and throat).

You have an instrument made of living muscle, bone and cartilage and other elastic tissues.

To produce a voice you need a blast of air, a vibrator and resonator.

- The air supply – the lungs – is in the chest.
- The vibrator – the vocal folds (cords) – are in the larynx or voice box in the neck.
- The resonating chamber, a very complicated one, includes the mouth, throat and sometimes the space behind and in the nose.

When your head is not positioned correctly over your shoulders, you are misaligning both the resonator and vibrator.

If your chin is tucked into your chest or tilted upwards, the vibrator is being squashed or pulled out of place.

Any changes in the spine and rib cage will alter the capacity and efficiency of your air supply.

Alignment is important

Good alignment and balance are the first steps to a better voice

Here are more self-assessment observations for you to make:

1. Look at yourself in a full-length mirror. Face the mirror and make a note of the following:
   (a) Is your head evenly balanced over your shoulders – or is it tilted slightly to right or left?
   (b) Are your shoulders balanced – or is one slightly higher than the other?
   (c) Is your torso slightly twisted to right or left?
   (d) Are your hips squarely facing front, or are they slightly twisted to right or left?

2. Turn your side to the mirror and turn only your head to look at yourself.
   (a) Is your head protruding in front of the rest of your body, or is your chin pushed into your neck?
   (b) Is there a nice line from your head to your tail or are there many exaggerated curves, particularly in the lower back?

3. Do you have a military stiffness or is your body flexible and flowing even when standing still?

4. Look at the illustration of efficient and balanced posture and compare it with yours. Are you close, or is there work to do?

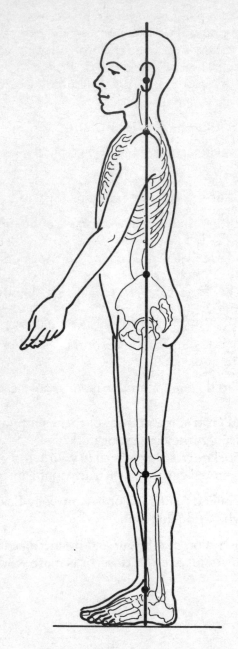

Illustration by Audrey Besterman

Efficient posture

One way of achieving a better voice is to use the most efficient posture. That means you are standing or sitting with balance and not muscular effort. The illustration shows balanced posture which is aided by gravity. Deviations from that posture indicate that extra muscles are habitually being called into play to keep you upright against the forces of gravity. The added energy being consumed then prevents you from enjoying the full benefit of other things you might wish to do, such as improving your voice, sports and dance.

Look carefully at the alignment of the body illustrated:

- The head is up with the eyes looking straight ahead.
- The ears are lined up with the point of the shoulder.
- The point of the shoulder is over the highest point of the hip.
- The hip is in line with the knee.
- The knee is in line with the front of the ankle.
- The weight is forward as if ready to move.
  (You may check whether your weight is forward by simply rising on your toes, maintaining a straight, *but not rigid* spine (without arching your back). If you have to move forward to be able to rise on your toes, you are much too far back on your heels.)

A mirror (at least three-quarter length) is *essential* to correcting your own posture. Always check your posture to see how it looks because it will feel strange to you until new patterns are established. It is valuable to have a friend to help you with this.

Correct posture begins with your head

A little experimentation will show you that the head cannot be lined up with the shoulders by tucking the chin into the neck or by tilting the head backwards. Here are a number of images that may be of use to you:

1. **Relax the muscles of the neck** by gently turning your head to the right, to the centre, to the left and centre again, several times. You can even add a gentle nod to the movement. Then

think of the head as a balloon floating upwards, taking the spine with it.

As the head moves upwards, imagine the whole spine lengthening and stretching.

2. **The head needs to be raised from the top.** Unfortunately, we have no muscles going towards the sky so take a tuft of hair on the crown of your head and gently pull the head towards the ceiling. Allow your head to move up with the hair and your spine to stretch gently upwards. (For those with minimal hair on the tops of their heads, take hold of the tops of your ears on either side and gently pull the head upwards – evenly. This will ensure that you do not do anything strange with your chin.)

3. **Think of the cheeks as having arrows** emerging from them that point straight ahead. (The arrows are parallel to the floor.)

As your head begins to move upwards you will find that the curves in your spine become less exaggerated, and the ear, shoulder and hips are in better alignment.

If you have a tendency to look dumpy, that will begin to change because your spine will be moving upwards away from your hips and you will no longer be sitting down into them.

Keep working at this. Eventually, as in the illustration, you should be able to drop an imaginary plumb line and have it fall through the crown of your head, ear, shoulder point, highest point of your hip bone, knees and in front of the ankle.

Keep in mind that when sitting, the alignment from head to hip is still important. Slumping while seated also takes too much energy.

It is too easy to sit at a desk and crumple. If you need to bend over your desk, remember to bend at the hips rather than humping your back and creating fatigue and possible back pain.

You may own one of the millions of chairs that make it impossible to sit well or comfortably. When the back of the chair does not allow you to sit straight, it is best to move forward, put

An important word about correcting yourself
The most important thing to do at the beginning of any kind
of self-correction, rehearsal or practice period is to

BECOME STILL

There is a very quick way to achieve this stillness:

- Sit in a chair.
- Place both feet on the floor.
- Make sure ten toes and both heels are touching the floor.
- Place ten fingers and palms of hands on something flat.
  The easiest way is to place your hands on your thighs.
  Your desk is all right if it is not too high. This exercise
  may be done standing if there is something on which to
  place the hands without straining the arms.

Maintain this contact and stillness for one minute. At first it
may feel strange, even difficult, to remain like this for just
30 seconds. However, for any changes to be effective the
body first needs to be still and quiet. Then you are ready to
work efficiently and effectively.

When such stillness is achieved, the body begins to let you
know the best way for it to function with less interference
from your mind, problems, etc.

In other words, allow your body to work *for* you rather
than against you.

both feet on the floor and allow the spine and head to move
upwards.

A special note about shoulders

Where are your shoulders?

- Are they up in a permanent shrug position?

- Are they held squarely and rigid – in an exaggerated military style?
- Are they curved inwards to protect yourself?

Don't force your shoulders backwards. If you do, that makes your back and neck poke forward. Think of them as moving away from the spine – in other words your shoulders are moving outwards and are getting wider. Allow your shoulders to flow away from your neck and back. Your arms will then hang freely. Your arms do not need to be held on to the shoulders. They will not fall off if the muscles relax.

Occasionally move your head to make sure that it and your neck are free and not held on to your spine.

Here are two *gentle* exercises for releasing your shoulders:

1. **Bring both shoulders up to your ears and release.** Do this 5 to 10 times while remembering to raise your shoulders (as in shrugging) rather than lower your ears or shorten your neck.

2. **Rotate your shoulders, first forwards, then backwards.** Do this gently rather than grinding your shoulder joint. Think of the shoulders as getting wider rather than narrower as you do this exercise.

Feel how your body is becoming taller and wider with nothing held rigidly or fixed. You will soon gain a sense of flowing and dynamic currents of energy running through every part of you. Remember that everything vibrates, including the body. If we hold on to anything – particularly posture – we stop the flow and ease of movement and voice.

Again, test your balance by rising on your toes from your stance. Remind yourself that the spine is straight, not curving backwards to create the balance that way.

Now you have the beginnings of an efficient vocal instrument. Try the words with which you began. They will sound vastly improved. You are now wasting no energy in maintaining your posture. You are balanced and only need to use your muscles for minor adjustments.

Let your body feel strange to you

Don't try to hold or fix the new posture but allow the body to find its own way.

At this point you may be feeling that you look strange and unnatural.

If your posture has been habitually poor, you will feel strange with new positions (remember how strange the stillness felt?) but you will not look odd. It is common to confuse what is NATURAL with what is HABITUAL. All the habits built into your posture during your lifetime are programmed into muscle computers. They are bound to complain at first. Don't listen! Instead listen to the improvement in your voice and feel the new ease of your body.

If you think you look peculiar, check your mirror and ask your friends. You will be surprised to find that not only do you look an inch taller, but your image is enhanced.

With your new efficient posture you will sense a renewed surge of energy and YOUR VOICE WILL REFLECT THIS.

This 'new you' can be achieved by picturing what you want, allowing it to happen, and not overworking. You probably pass a number of mirrors or reflectors during the day. Just sneak a little look at yourself as you go by them.

2. Breathing

There is no life, let alone voice, without air!
Continuous, free air flow is critical for a resonant, free voice
and good health.

In addition to a better voice, the benefits of breathing properly
include better circulation, freedom from tension in the chest,
lungs that function more efficiently, and a look of ease, particularly a lack of tension in the neck and face.

Note. A balanced alignment is essential for efficient breathing.

Here are some suggestions for checking the efficiency of your
own patterns of breathing. Experiment in front of a mirror.

1. Take a big breath and watch carefully. One of several things
   may happen:
   (a) Your chest comes up.
   (b) Your head looks as if it is sinking into your shoulders.
   (c) The outlines of the muscles in your neck begin to show.
   Breathe out gently.

2. Place your finger on your Adam's apple (larynx) which is part
   of the voice box. Now take a breath.
      Does the larynx move up or down?
   (a) If your throat relaxes as you breathe, the larynx moves
        downwards.
   (b) If you are tense, it may move upwards towards the jaw
        bone as in swallowing.

3. Take another deep breath.
      Observe the way in which your abdomen moves.
   (a) If it moves in, you are inhibiting your own breathing.

(b) If it moves out, you are on the right track.

(c) If it does not move at all, you are far too tense and probably using only your shoulders to help you take in air.

4. Lastly, put your hands around your lower ribs towards your back and take a breath.

Is there any movement there? It is far better if there is.

Efficient breathing for the best use of your voice

Here are some guidelines to help you understand efficient breathing. Exercises to help you are given on page 23.

1. More than half the work of efficient breathing is already done if the body is properly aligned.

2. The activity of breathing is best seen mainly in the movement of the lower ribs, back, and upper abdomen. Letting the abdomen balloon outwards is unsightly and unnecessary. Any breathing done by raising the shoulders and upper chest tenses the neck and inhibits the larynx.

3. The muscles of the abdomen and lower ribs should be sufficiently relaxed to allow them to move freely in and out with the breath.

4. **Breathing in** – inhalation
When you inhale, the space inside the chest increases because the diaphragm contracts downwards and the lower ribs and abdomen expand.

The bigger the breath, the more expansion is needed.

Note. If the abdomen is tightly held, the lower ribs and diaphragm cannot move sufficiently and the air supply has to be augmented by lifting the upper chest – not very efficient for the best use of the voice.

5. **Breathing out** – exhalation
When you exhale, the diaphragm relaxes upwards and the muscles of the abdomen contract towards the spine.

Note. It is very important that you maintain your good

alignment because control of your outgoing air is lost if you allow yourself to crumple or your chest to collapse.

6. Obvious tension in the face, neck or chest, and audible sound on inhalation are all indications of stressful breathing. If the chest is tight you will feel as though you are already full of air. Then, when you begin to speak or sing, you will find that you do not have enough breath – a real 'catch 22' situation! If there is audible sound, it is an indication that your throat is too tense as you breathe.

Reminder. Observe your breathing during the exercise for becoming still. You will find that it seems easy and natural. It is especially important to become still when you begin to correct your own patterns of breathing in the exercises that follow.

Correcting your own pattern of breathing is easier than you think!

Here are some suggestions:

1. Lie on the floor, knees bent, feet flat on the floor; use several books to support your head, and simply become aware of your breathing pattern. (This is also an excellent way of relaxing after a hard day's work as well as relieving tension in the muscles of the back.)
   (a) Put one hand on your abdomen and one on your chest. Make sure the chest remains still while the abdomen and lower ribs move in and out.
   (b) Increase the depth of your breathing making the abdomen and lower ribs more and more active. Again, do not allow the chest to interfere.
   On the IN BREATH allow the abdomen, lower ribs and back to expand.
   On the OUT BREATH allow the muscles of the abdomen, rather than the chest, to do the work. They should move towards your spine or the floor.

2. Sit in a chair (or cross-legged on the floor) in a good alignment:

(a) Blow out all the air you can, and help the process by pulling your abdomen in towards your spine.
(b) When you think you have blown out all your air, get rid of a bit more (you will find you had more than you thought).
(c) Without altering the position of your chest, release your abdomen – the air will rush back in. Note where this is happening – the lower rib area.
(d) Repeat this pattern until your coordination is consistent and you will soon find the action of your breathing has moved downwards.

3. Sit on the edge of a chair with both feet flat on the floor; let your body fold over your legs and *allow the arms to hang freely and the head to hang relaxed.*

   As you breathe in and out you can feel the movement of the abdomen, lower ribs and back.

   This is a good way to experience the proper sensation so that you have a guideline when sitting or standing.

4. Stand up and clasp your hands together, stretching your arms above your head. Your palms should be facing the ceiling and your head up, not pushed forward.

   Now follow the directions for Exercise 2.
   With the arms and shoulders fixed in this position, you are forced to use your abdominal muscles.

   When you are confident of the correct feeling, release your arms and do the same thing in a normal standing position.

5. If you are at work and conscious of being watched, here are some additional ideas.
   (a) When sitting, make sure your lower back is against the chair.
   (b) Use the back of the chair as well as your spine as a guide.
   (c) As you breathe in, feel your body expand to meet the chair.
   (d) As you breathe, pull your stomach muscles towards the back of the chair.

6. One final suggestion, using your belt or waistband as a guidepost:
   (a) Hook your fingers around your belt.
   (b) As you breathe in, pull your belt out with the idea of filling the space.
   (c) As you breathe out, push your belt inwards while thinking of narrowing the area within your belt.

These exercises give you an idea of the physical process of efficient breathing. With diligent attention, the patterns you have been practising become good habits which take little thought. In other words, they begin to become natural.

The most important thing is to keep breathing. This directive may seem obvious; however, one of the most prevalent problems in speaking is that people manage to stop breathing in order to speak. Psychologists will also tell you that people react to surprise, shock, trauma and other situations by holding their breath. This immediately stops the flow of breath and the natural vibratory pattern of the body.

3. Sound Is Made by the Vocal Folds

The vocal folds (otherwise known as the vocal cords) are like two shelves made up of muscles, a small piece of cartilage and other elastic membranes and ligaments. They are located in the larynx which sits at the top of the windpipe (trachea). These folds act first as a protector of your lungs by keeping out foreign matter, and second as your source of vocal sound.

You have probably already had some experience with the protective aspect. Normally, when you swallow, the vocal folds close tightly to prevent food entering the lungs. However, if you have ever tried to talk and eat at the same time, you may have had the unpleasant experience of something going 'down the wrong way'. The resultant gagging represented the protective forces of your vocal folds at work.

When you wish to make sound, air comes from the lungs through the vocal folds. They close – or move closer together – and begin to vibrate. You can get an idea of how this works by blowing up a balloon and then stretching the mouth of it. The squeal that follows is distantly related to the way the vocal folds function.

How the vocal folds come together is of some importance to the quality of sound emitted, and very often related to the ease with which you breathe.

The breathy voice

When the vocal folds do not come together adequately, a breathy sound is heard. This is usually caused by a combination of poor posture, faulty breathing and lack of energy.

Is your voice breathy or weak? If so, do the following exercise (use a tape recorder):

1. Check your posture and breathing in a mirror.

2. Turn your head to the right or left and breathe in. Return your head to centre and say HEE or HAY as you breathe out. Do this in rhythm at a moderately fast pace and alternate breathing in to the right and left. *Note.* Air is always expelled to the centre.

3. Using the same vowels and head motions say a series of sounds on one breath, eg HEE-HEE-HEE-HEE-HEE or a sentence like 'Hello, how are you' or 'My name is ...'.

4. As you do this exercise, imagine your body getting taller and wider as you make sound. This will prevent you from collapsing into your body as you speak.

5. Use full voice for this exercise. Using air efficiently means using balanced energy.

The breath-saver's voice

The opposite of a voice that is too breathy is one that is too tight or tense. The characteristic sound of this type of voice tends to be harsh or strident. The problem is that too little air is being used. Many people speak (and especially sing) as if they are being very stingy with their breath and are not willing to share it. Often this faulty thinking has to do with our old notions of not having enough air or attempting to control the breath. The result is tension in the neck and chest, and vocal folds that are nearly paralysed.

Reminder. There is no sound without air.

Correcting this problem means allowing more air to come through as we speak. At first it will sound very breathy inside your head, but persevere because others will not hear it that way. If you have trouble believing this, use your tape recorder.

You will have enough air. You will also get used to hearing a buzzier sound in your head. That sound is indicative of a warmer vocal quality with much more freedom. Just remember the idea of 'controlling' or holding back breath is devastating to vocal freedom.

A special note about the glottal stop

Some people use what are called glottal stops in producing sound. (The glottis is the opening between the vocal folds.) You can feel what this is like for yourself:

1. Hold your breath. Your vocal folds will close tightly to prevent air escaping.
2. Now say a word beginning with a vowel, for example, each, every, all.

What happens?
An explosion. The vocal folds literally have to burst apart to make the sound. The pressure from the stopped-up air beneath the vocal folds comes bursting out. This is not healthy for the voice and also contributes a certain harshness to vocal quality.

These sounds can be heard in strong Cockney or Australian accents where a word like 'twenty' becomes 'twen-ee'.

The 't' is dropped and replaced by something like a grunt.

It is also common to hear this sound in Germanic languages, especially before words beginning with a vowel.

The glottal stop shocks the vocal folds. Such a manner of vocal attack is potentially harmful to the vocal folds because these habits can irritate the edges of the folds (even cause growths) and make the voice sound hoarse.

Suggestions for easily produced sound

Sound is best made with the air moving easily through the throat. Air moves in a continuous cycle with no obvious gap between the in and out patterns.

1. **First become still.**

2. **Observe your relaxed breathing pattern.** Do not alter it. Just observe. By this time you are breathing mainly in the area of the lower ribs, back and abdomen, aren't you?

   While you are observing, imagine your head being easily movable and floating upwards and the neck, shoulders and face relaxed (but not flaccid or immovable).

3. **When the breathing feels easy** – almost silky – let a sound start to come as you breathe out. This sound can be just a gentle and short Hum. Allow this sound to begin at the point where the in breath becomes the out breath. For the purposes of this exercise, do not allow the breath to hold momentarily, even for a split second.

   Do this for a while until you feel the sound vibrating through much of your body and the spaces of your throat. Don't force the sound, just allow it to release itself from you.

4. **Now let the jaw relax downwards** (don't pull it down) – all the while repeating the Hum. As you open your mouth the syllable will probably become Mah. Keep the silkiness of breath and sound.

5. **When you consistently feel an easy, buzzing sound** that fills your throat, head (figuratively speaking) and body, add other vowels such as Mee, Moh, Moo or Hah, Hee, Hoh, Hoo until they all feel vibrant. (Use a tape recorder to check the consistency of your quality.)

6. **Now add words to this Hum.**
   Hummm How are you?
   Hummm My name is—.
   Choose any conversation you wish but start each new phrase after a breath with the Hummmmmm.

7. **When you become comfortable with all the above,** allow the sound to become continuous. It will seem a bit like sing-song but stick with it.

8. **For those who wish to sing, now is the time.** Sing any words, keeping the buzz or shimmery feeling. Forget the 'idea' of singing, just allow this easy feeling of continual sound to

emerge. (Somehow people have been programmed to think of singing as doing something and that usually involves tension.)

4. Vocal Quality and Resonance

What if the flute and cello mentioned earlier were made of a soft, rubbery material? You can imagine all the distortions in the quality of the sound as the shapes of those instruments change.

This is exactly what happens to the *vocal resonator* (the throat and mouth) which is made of muscle that is constantly moving into various shapes and formations. No wonder each voice is unique! And, to add to that difference, we all have our various habits of speech derived from our family background, local and regional environments.

For a moment imitate someone you know who has a distinctive voice. Repeat the exercise several times so that you notice what you are doing with your mouth, throat, tongue and face to make those sounds. Your imitation is probably an exaggeration of what that person does on a daily basis to make sound.

In order to make sound you simply build in certain muscular patterns. These patterns become 'programmed' by your muscle computers and when others describe your voice they may comment on accent or dialect and use words such as pleasant, harsh, sweet, strident and other nice or not-so-nice terms.

Emotions are apparent in the voice

Not only do various muscular patterns alter the quality of sound but the emotions play a very large role too. You have often noticed when a friend is feeling well or unwell just by the sound of the voice. Emotions can cause subconscious changes in the way you make sound and alter the quality – sometimes without your knowledge. This is why we are able to give a double message or meaning to what we are saying without intending to do so.

The quality of a voice can be deliberately changed by altering something physical or by the imagination (thinking of an emotion).

To develop a better understanding of how this works, allow yourself to play some games with vocal quality. For this you will need a mirror, a tape recorder and, if you are trusting and brave, a partner with whom you can do the exercises that follow.

The rules are:
Use a firm voice.
No inhibitions – be daring.
No self-criticism.
Especially no critical listening.
Lose yourself in the fun and enjoy yourself.

Choose a line of simple prose or a line of a poem, the words 'Hello, how are you,' or something else that is easy. You are going to use the same words each time in the ways listed below.

First, here is a checklist of areas to observe:

1. your face
2. your eyes
3. your mouth and lips
4. your tongue
5. your throat and jaw
6. your chest
7. your whole body
8. the sound itself.

Now follow these directions with your chosen words.

Say your text with full voice:

1. happily
2. sadly
3. really depressed
4. exultantly or exuberantly
5. as in everyday conversation

6. as if speaking in a large room
7. as if speaking in a large auditorium
8. as if you are a 'ham' actor.

If you are really daring, sing your words:

1. like a lullaby
2. as if in the bath or shower
3. in the style of a rock singer
4. in the style of a country and western singer
5. in the style of musical theatre
6. in the manner of a grand opera singer.

You have probably found, to your surprise, that you have been able to do most of the list without any trouble. There are many things you have observed such as facial mannerisms, tensions around the face and mouth, and distortion in the sounds.

Now, notice the people around you. You will find that the exaggerations you were using to make those various sounds are prominent in everyday life.

Have a good look and observe all the extra muscular tensions people use to speak or, even worse, to sing!

A good rule to follow is:

If it looks distorted, it will probably sound distorted!

If you need examples, here are some that are readily available.

1. **TV newscasters**
   Observe the wrinkled brows, tense mouths and lips. Many people seem to furrow their brows as they read. It isn't necessary to make sound with the aid of the brows.

2. **People who appear shy**
   Many of them look as if they would rather inhale their words than exhale them. Notice the lips; they are probably pulled inwards as if trying to keep the sound from coming out.

3. **Members of choirs**
   (a) Sopranos with a constant smile (for brightness?)
   (b) Altos with lips covering the teeth (they hear it bigger

inside their heads this way but the audience only hears muddy tone)

(c) Tenors with chins up towards the ceiling (high notes are not found on the ceiling)

(d) Basses with their chins tucked or jammed into their chests (some look for their low notes there).

Note. All the characteristics seen in the choir are also apparent in the person on the street. There is always someone who manages to say: 'I am sad', with a smile or to speak with the chin in the air or down in the chest.

4. Actors and singers on TV
Can you name the muscles and veins? Is the jaw distorted to the right or left or the mouth over opened? This doesn't just happen in character parts. Often it is tension.

5. The dead face syndrome
This is the person who speaks without moving a facial muscle (some type of control?). The effect is either a monotonous, colourless sound or one which is pushed into the nose.

6. The important person syndrome
This person tries to sound impressive by obviously changing his voice – usually adding throat and tongue tension so the voice has either a metallic ring or sounds garbled.

7. The constant smile syndrome
The smiling, overly sweet lady to whom you would like to give a swift kick in order to get to the real person. The result of the constant smile is a superficial sound – surely not what the person intends.

8. The 'determined' jaw
This makes a person look angry and sound tense. Try it yourself. Push your jaw forward and speak like that for a few minutes. You will begin to seem angry to yourself.

The list is endless. As you can see, there are many ways to observe visible (to say nothing of invisible) tensions which affect the quality of your voice.

Removing obvious, visible tension and mannerisms will improve your vocal quality

You may not hear the difference immediately in yourself but others will. They will not say to you, 'Oh, you have changed your voice'. It will not be that obvious. They are far more likely to say that something about you has changed or that you are somehow different.

You are the only one who knows exactly what you are working to achieve and what in particular you are changing. No one really exaggerates enough for others to pick out the particular differences. Therefore you do not have to be self-conscious about your own reforms. These differences may seem mountainous to you, but to the observer they are barely perceptible. So be daring!

Changing your vocal quality

If you are changing mannerisms you must use a mirror. Simply to *think* of making the change is not enough to do the job. Remember that you have already programmed your muscle computers another way and the old habits will take over every time. So I repeat, use the mirror and do look at yourself. It may help to imagine that it is not you, but some employee or member of staff who you are observing and correcting.

It is also useful to record your practice so that you can be more objective about any changes. The tape recorder will help you to convince yourself that you have not changed nearly as much as it sounds to you inside your head.

As mentioned in the Foreword, the acoustics of the throat and vocal tract play tricks on you – that is, you sound different on tape or to others from the way you do to yourself. So you have to learn to hear your voice as others do – not as you sound to yourself inside your head. This is the most difficult aspect of changing your voice, whether it be speech or singing!

To begin:

1. Make a list of visible tensions and mannerisms you would like to erase.

2. Choose one a week.

3. Recite passages in front of a mirror to make sure you look the way you wish.

4. Use your tape recorder to check the quality.

5. Remind yourself of your goal by leaving notes in obvious places. For example, put notes on your telephone, mirror, desk, etc. You might have notes everywhere saying 'Open your mouth' or what you feel needs the most work.

Do not listen to yourself critically

It is possible to change your vocal quality but you must not listen and analyse as you do it. You will ruin it if you are not spontaneous. If you want to hear the sound, use your tape recorder. By listening and making the sound at the same time you stop the flow and spontaneity and cause the muscles to hold momentarily. This adds tension, the very thing you do not want! Imagine or visualise what you want, the feel, the sound, the quality, then allow it to happen. If it is not satisfactory, do it again – do not stop it in midstream!

5. Making Your Voice More Powerful

Speaking with power means using more energy and space, not more tension.

Speakers often wonder how opera singers make such big sounds. They do it by enlarging the space in the throat and mouth and using more air. The throat will respond naturally to your demands when you are free of tension.

The confusion about space and power arises from the paradoxical perceptions we get from the throat. When the throat is tense, it can be more satisfying because it feels as if something is happening. There is – tension. When there is adequate space and release, there is the feeling that nothing is happening.

This sensation is so subtle that it makes people want to add pressure in the throat – the opposite of what is needed. While experimenting with this concept of space you may feel as if you have lost control. Good! In this work you have to lose control to gain it. Dare to feel a bit lost with it all.

> When you are free of tension, the throat will respond naturally and an easily produced vocal quality will emerge.

This is a dictum everyone can use – speakers and every type of singer. Some people think that powerful singing comes from a secret catacomb deep in the body. It comes from the same place as speech and is governed by the same rules. The confusion comes from trying to take everyday conversational speaking and relate it to something like singing opera where much more carrying power and volume are needed.

Remember the exercises in Chapter 4? These were designed to produce bigger and bigger voice and sound. If the sound you are using needs to fill a large hall or be heard over an orchestra, of course something more is necessary.

The bigger the sound, the more space is needed in the throat (much like yawning or sounding 'pompous' to yourself inside). Also, you will need more air and energy. One suggestion is to think of inhaling (gently) your audience. You will then accommodate everyone no matter what the size of your group.

To summarise, a powerful voice is the product of good alignment, efficient use of air, a throat that freely responds and enlarges, and energy that is properly directed.

Experiment with this concept of more space inside your throat and mouth.

Note. I repeat: space does not mean tension. If you feel a lot happening, it is likely to be tension. When you feel as if nothing is happening, you are more likely to be on the right track.

Begin by yawning. At the beginning of a yawn there is a large amount of space in the mouth and throat. Actually speak or sing-song into that space. It will seem very strange at first, but it is richer, fuller and has carrying power. (This is where you are not allowed to listen and criticise yourself. It does sound ridiculous inside you at first.)

An ordinary yell will not carry as far because there is so much constriction in the throat. A yell will also strain the voice.

However, if you make a big, fat, almost pompous sound, it will carry.

Note. This same approach will help you if you need to speak in a large room without the aid of a microphone.

Using a microphone

You may be asking why you cannot use a microphone to make your voice bigger. The microphone cannot make your voice bigger, it can only amplify what you put into it. It will not change the sound of your voice, but it is possible for the sound to be distorted if it is of poor quality or if it is used improperly.

The job of the microphone is to carry the voice – as it is – to the speaker system so that a person can be heard. So all your good qualities and faults will be magnified for everyone to hear. Think of your voice as being put under a microscope. None of the cells changes – they are simply made to look larger so that more detail can be seen. Do you want your voice, as it is, to be put under a microscope?

The microphone is there to amplify, so there is no need to yell into it or swallow it. This only distorts the sound. You need only remind yourself of labouring to decipher public announcements in railway stations and public buildings to understand this fully.

Speak firmly and comfortably. The microphone will do the rest. The best way to use the mike is to ignore it. Forget that it is there! If you feel you must stay close, adjust it so that your mouth is several inches away. The closer you are, the more distorted the sound.

Test the mike by speaking. Don't tap or blow on it.

Breathe in through the nose when using a mike because it is quieter. If a gasping breath is taken, it can be very annoying for the audience.

It is always advisable to arrive early to test sound systems. Fiddling with the microphone can be annoying to an audience and waste valuable time. There are also several types of mike in common use and it is helpful to know whether you need to stand close or some distance away.

6. Words, Diction and Ideas

If you have followed closely all that has gone before, your diction is probably already much improved, no matter what your accent or dialect. The object is not to change your accent (unless you wish) but to allow it to be clearly understood. Regional accents are your heritage, often charming, and add great colour and variety to speech patterns. However, you may find the following information helpful.

Words are formed by the throat, mouth, jaw, teeth and lips.

Vowels are shaped in the throat and in the mouth by various positions of the tongue, soft palate and lips.

Note. The vowels are made more by the tongue than by the lips except for the OH and OO.

Most people exaggerate the AY and EE by pulling the lips wide into a smile. This brightens the quality of those vowels and distorts them in comparison to the other vowels you pronounce.

Say all the vowels in front of a mirror and note what happens to your lips when you say AY and EE.
Do your lips change drastically into a smile?
Don't allow this to happen but instead allow the jaw to relax downwards, leave the lips alone and the tongue will then do the work it is designed to do.

Consonants are formed by the action of the tongue, palate, lips and teeth. Relaxed tongue and lips work far more efficiently and clearly than ones that are tense or exaggerating movements. Some people will speak very easily on a one-to-one basis; however, when they are in front of a group they begin to distort the lips and exaggerate the tongue movement to ensure clarity. It is not necessary and is often unsightly and abnormal looking. If this is the case, you can be sure the sound is affected and the quality poorer for it.

Specific details of elocution can be found in any book on phonetics and represent a depth which is beyond the scope of this book.

Relaxed lips, tongue, and jaw allow clear, easy pronunciation.

Understanding someone's speech can be difficult when the effort the speaker is making causes physical distortions, particularly distortions of the jaw, lips and tongue.

Experience the following for yourself (use your tape recorder for this one).

While saying the words, 'Hello, how are you?':

1. **Move the jaw from side to side or forwards and backwards.**
   It is obvious that the words sound chewed.
   Now just allow your jaw to move up and down loosely – the words become much clearer. If the jaw is frozen or held tightly the words will be muffled and the diction muddy.

2. **Pull your lips over your teeth.**
   Again, this muffles the sound.
   Lips are fleshy and absorb sound – much like a wedge of meat being put into the bell of a horn. It would not sound clear if covered in that manner. Neither do people. (Some singers do this thinking they are making a big sound. Unfortunately, it is only big inside their heads.)

3. **Hold the tongue tensely or rigidly as you speak.**
   The sound becomes garbled and artificial sounding.
   Do this again with a relaxed tongue, letting the tip remain near the lower front teeth. It will sound much clearer. Go back to your tape recorder for confirmation.

4. **Speak through clenched teeth.**
   This sounds angry, even furious.
   So many people do this and do not understand why it is that others mistakenly think they are angry.

Relax the jaw and open your mouth when you speak. Your mouth is open enough when there is at least some space showing between the upper and lower teeth.

A word about the 's'

As you say an s, watch your tongue in the mirror. The hiss part is made with the tip of the tongue in the centre of the mouth at the front teeth. The air comes out directly in the middle.

When the tongue deviates to the left or right and air comes out on the side, there is a lisp – a common speech defect that few bother to correct. Often this is because adults think it is a cute habit in young children.

Ers and ums

Silence while you are thinking is all right. What seems like a long time to you is really very short for your audience. To fill a speech with 'ers' and 'ums' interrupts the flow of thought and makes the concepts and ideas difficult to find. Tell yourself that you can be comfortable with silence. Has anyone ever walked out on you in mid-sentence or while you were thinking between phrases? Audiences usually stay until the speaker finishes.

Making sense of your ideas

It is important to make beautiful sounds; however, these sounds must flow into ideas that make sense if your message is to be heard and understood. An excellent text can be ruined by a poor reading and a speech can be difficult to comprehend if delivered badly. How often have you heard a talk, or particularly a lecture, in which the speaker paused every three or four words for emphasis? For example:

A very important aspect / of communication / is speaking / in whole ideas.

Rather than:

A very important aspect of communication is speaking in whole ideas.

A listener will remember what he or she hears when presented with a whole concept rather than disjointed phrases. When someone speaks in short phrases, the outline of the sentence and the thought disappear. The responses to such delivery are misunderstanding, boredom, loss of sales and possibly loud snoring in the back of the room.

For speech to flow, it must have a sense of rhythm and phrasing. A speech given with a prepared text can be practised. An impromptu talk or speech without notes is more difficult to rehearse; however, once the sense of rhythm is understood, it is easily incorporated.

Here is a way to master the rhythm and flow of ideas in speaking:

1. **Underscore the important words of your text as if you were sending a telegram.**
   A passage has been underscored for you as an example.

   A free <u>body responds</u> to the world around it <u>with</u> minute

   <u>adjustments</u> of alignment and poise <u>according to</u> the

   physical, emotional or mental <u>situation of</u> the <u>moment</u>.

   <u>It is</u> a constantly changing responsive <u>mechanism that</u> can

   <u>ensure clarity</u> of voice, <u>correct</u> vocal <u>adjustment</u>, <u>breath</u>

   <u>flow</u> and a <u>dynamic rhythm</u> which is <u>sensitive to</u> the

   momentary <u>thoughts and feelings of</u> the <u>speaker</u>.

It is better to underscore only a few words at first. You can add more later if they are really necessary. Most people tend to underscore far too many. Make this a 'cheap' telegram.

2. **Now read your text aloud, moving through to the underscored words.**

   Think of the sentence as a whole rather than various short phrases. After reading a passage aloud several times you will find that the rhythm of the words will begin to flow.

   It is especially important to use a tape recorder for this practice.

3. **If you do not use a prepared text you can still practise by underscoring any passage of an article or even a poem.** This kind of practice will enable you to get the feel of the rhythm and flow. Reading poetry aloud is also helpful. Just remember to read the whole sentence of the poem rather than only to the end of each line. Poetry can become extremely dull if the end of each line finishes with a rhythmic thump.

4. **All types of presentation need rhythm and flow**, even a company report. In fact, by looking at a company report or similar type of document in this way, you may find that it needs to be written in a more interesting format. There is no need for any presentation ever to be dull. Why give it orally at all if it is merely a formality? In this case it would be better to give it out in written form.

Your face and eyes are special keys to communication

The ideas you are expressing when you speak need your full involvement and commitment. Your audience will be judging you by your voice, your body language and especially your face. Your face can say it all. Yet so many people 'turn out the light' in their faces and eyes because they are thinking – or analysing simultaneously – as they attempt to communicate. This has the effect of stopping all that necessary vibration and balance of spontaneous energy mentioned earlier.

The habit of analysing, listening to yourself or self-criticism completely stops the process of communication and often gives the wrong intent or meaning to the message. When this happens, there are words which do not seem to match the intended meaning. This is where the idea of 'mixed messages' arises.

47

A face can be deadpan – with immovable cheeks and eyes – or it can always have a fixed smile. Both affect sound. One is boring and without colour, the other overly bright and shallow.

Speak spontaneously, without effort and without over-thinking. Say it. Mean it. Allow your face and eyes to show it. And, above all, let your eyes reflect the YOU inside. Then the message is clear and honest.

A word about hands

The question is often asked: 'What do I do with my hands?'

The answer is: 'What do you do with them in your normal everyday speech?'

In our daily life we use our hands quite unconsciously. It is only when we get up to speak that we become aware of them. So what do we do? We fix them somewhere – either by our sides, crossed in front, over the solar plexus or over the pubic area. Just remember: wherever you place your hands will cause your audience to focus attention on that spot.

When you are uncertain about what to do with your hands, put them gently (if the knuckles turn white, it is not gentle) on the podium or desk, or let them hang by your side and allow your face to do the talking. Feel free to use your hands. You do it all day with ease.

Summary notes on speaking and presenting

1. **Just prior to your presentation sit quietly and mentally prepare your message.** Have several (not more than two or three) main points in mind – no more. If you are clear on these points, other information will flow.

2. **When presenting, stand or sit 'tall',** have your weight a little forward, be flexible, not stiff, and allow your hands to relax and be used normally. You body language is important.

3. **Speak clearly and firmly.** Ask anyone in the audience or group to inform you if they cannot hear or understand you.

4. **Allow your face and eyes to show your enthusiasm.** A 'thinking' face creates the impression that the speaker is not there, therefore contact with the audience can be lost.

5. **If you are reading material, make sure you are facing forward** and your face is visible to your audience. A face looking downwards sends sound into the floor.

6. **When using a board or flip-chart, first state what you are about to write while facing forward,** then write it and repeat it if necessary. Do not talk to the board.

7. **Speak in whole ideas and thoughts** rather than chopped phrases. For example:
   I am speaking on behalf of men and women in management.

   Not:
   I am speaking / on behalf / of men and women / in management.

   There is no need to pause before prepositional phrases. Pick out the important words to emphasise and do not add many pauses as this causes the listener to lose the main thread of thought.

8. **Omit all extraneous sounds,** such as um and er, or any words repeated without meaning such as I hope, in fact, really, etc. Silence is all right. People will wait for you to think. It may seem like hours to you but is only milliseconds.

9. **Speak to your audience as if they are your friends** and they will be.

10. **And finally,** remind yourself often of the message on page 50.

To speak well and clearly

Relax.*

Your face (but not deadpan)
Your tongue
Your jaw
Your lips

Keep your cheeks alive
Let your eyes sparkle
Have conviction about what you are saying
Be yourself

AND YOU WILL BE FINE!

* *Note.* Relaxation does not mean becoming droopy or lifeless but refers to a balance of energies. It also means no mannerisms or distortions. They are unnecessary for any normal speech.

7. Audiences and Nerves

The word 'audience' in this book means anyone who is listening to you whether it is one or a thousand. You are confronted with many types of audience and meetings on a daily basis: family, friends, colleagues, customers, sales force, board, students, business, social, club, etc. The list is endless. Each of these speaking situations will affect you differently and you will probably feel the need to vary your approach with each type of audience.

The techniques you have been given are useful and important any time you speak. However, there are other important considerations such as the type of person(s) to whom you will speak, how many, the environment – noisy, acoustically dull, boardroom, office, large auditorium. All these factors will affect your perception more than their reception of your presentation. Therefore it is important for you to know as much as possible beforehand and to practise with that in mind.

The real difference in speaking before groups is your concept of size. Obviously, if the group is small you do not want to shout at them. On the other hand, a large audience needs exaggeration. It is this aspect that presents many people with problems.

Think of actors on a stage. If they use small voices and small actions, the audience will not get the message. The same is true of speaking in public. There is a point where we all become actors, and it is important. Surely you are speaking in order to make a sale, convince someone of something, or make a point. Then why undersell yourself or your product?

Presentation checklist

It might be useful for you to answer the following questions for yourself each time you make a presentation or speak.

1. How many people am I addressing?

2. What is the environment?
   - (a) Office – whose?
   - (b) What is the size of the room?
   - (c) Am I going to be behind a desk, a table, a lectern?
     Most important, do I want to be behind anything?
     Do I want a barrier between me and this particular audience?
     Or do I need a place to put notes?
   - (d) Is my presentation being taped or videoed?
   - (e) Am I speaking to the media – press, radio, TV?
     Do I need make-up or special clothes?

3. What equipment do I need?
   - (a) Something on which to write – what?
   - (b) Microphone, tape recorder, video, screen, overhead projector, other?
   - (c) Do I need anyone to help me?

4. Will I need handouts, other written preparations?

5. Who will introduce me?
   Am I prepared to introduce myself?

6. Have I practised my presentation both by visualisation and speaking it?

7. Am I enthusiastic about my subject?

8. If I have paid attention to all the above, why am I nervous?

Overcoming nervousness

Getting excited about being interviewed or speaking before an audience is very normal and healthy because it increases your awareness. However, excessive nervousness is caused by forgetting the reason for speaking.

The message is the most important aspect of communication, even if it is about yourself (for example, an interview). If the message is uppermost then you will only interfere with it if you begin to worry about yourself – how do I look, are my hands shaking, what if I forget? If you have time to ask yourself these questions while you are speaking, you most certainly have forgotten your topic and your reason for being there.

If a speaker is self-conscious the audience will sense this and its attention will be directed towards the person (and the habits being exhibited) rather than the message. Think of it this way:

SPEAKER ————> <u>MESSAGE</u> <———— AUDIENCE

When the speaker is completely committed to the message, the audience also will focus on it.

Once the speaker begins to think or worry about himself/herself, the audience will follow suit and miss the message.

```
    *  *  *
* SPEAKER *  <—————————————————— AUDIENCE
    *  *  *              message
```

At this point communication is lost. It can be regained. However, valuable points may have been lost and time has elapsed.

* Represents a 'speaker-worry'.

Positive action

Replace all those worries and negative thoughts with very definite things to do. Make a simple checklist and follow it. These suggestions have already appeared in earlier chapters; remind yourself of them now:

1. **Become still.** This is the most important thing you can do for yourself. Once you do this, you are able to think much more clearly.

2. **Follow your breathing pattern.**

3. **Write reminders to yourself** on top of your manuscript or list of notes.

4. **Use the list of questions in this chapter.**

5. **Practise.** If you should be asked to speak extemporaneously, your previous practice for other talks will have provided valuable habits for you. Before you know it, your reactions to speaking will be spontaneous.

6. **Maintain your enthusiasm for your subject.** If you are truly lost in your topic, you will have no time to think or worry about yourself. Remember, you are the expert at that time. No one but you knows what you are going to say.

7. **Begin your talk or speech by looking at your audience.** This is particularly important when you are reading it. Many speakers have said 'Good morning' or 'Good evening' to their notes and lost the audience immediately. If you are using a card with two or three main points, there is no excuse for not looking at your audience.

8. **Talk to your audience as if they are your friends.**

8. Practising and Caring for Your Voice

Any new skill demands a certain amount of practice and it is the quality of practice that determines the rate of progress. Time is precious, so the more efficient your practice, the less time you need. When you are learning new skills many short practices are more helpful than one long one. *And this is possible within the work situation.*

1. **Your first goal is to become still** – ten toes on the floor and ten fingers on something flat or your thighs. This can be done while you are listening also. It is one of the best ways to calm yourself or slow down if things are becoming too much for you.

2. **Work only for short periods** (as little as two or three minutes), but do so several times a day. When you are correcting old patterns and habits it can be tedious and boring. You can keep that from happening by having a short practice.

3. **Choose only ONE thing to correct at a time**, and be patient and painstaking about it. One way to create confusion is to set too many goals for yourself. Give yourself a break. Set an attainable goal for each practice period. By working on one thing at a time you actually learn faster. You will find that, as you work on each thing for a day, a week even, it becomes habit and you can forget it and go on to something else.

4. **Many reminders are essential** because you are creating new habits. Leave notes for yourself on your lecture notes, desk, mirror, telephone, dashboard of your car, wardrobe door, or any place your eyes might stray during the day. (Those little

note pads with sticky tops are very useful. You can put them everywhere without damaging anything.)

5. **Put this into practice by reading aloud** a passage of your choice several times a day, and remind yourself again about the task for the day or the practice period.

6. **Do not tire your voice or your mind by practising too long.** Remember your vocal instrument is made of muscles, and functions like other parts of the body. It can get tired and therefore does not need hours of hard work.

7. **Practise by visualising what you want to happen.** Become *still* and go through the exercise mentally. Experience the feelings in your throat and body and the sound and the interpretation. Then ALLOW rather than DO. (If 10 times is good, 100 is NOT better in this case.) It is the quality of the practice and efficiency of energy that are important.

Some hints on caring for your new voice

Be kind to your vocal instrument.

1. **Talking too loudly or yelling needlessly abuses the voice.** The only replacements available for the voice are mechanical and do not sound very good.

2. **Refrain from talking over noise** at a disco, on the tube, a busy street, or while watching TV. Have you ever noticed how hoarse your voice is after a party?

3. **When your voice is hoarse**, for whatever reason – laryngitis, colds, strain or your own fatigue – TALK LESS, OR NOT AT ALL THAT DAY, and certainly avoid singing (especially in the pub).

   If you have no voice, laryngitis or a severe sore throat, DO NOT USE YOUR VOICE AT ALL! It is sick. You can put a plaster cast on a broken ankle but unfortunately not on a 'broken' voice. See your doctor and REST YOUR VOICE!

4. **If you do have a cold or voice problems,** you can help yourself

by keeping your throat moist – a lozenge, steam, and drinking plenty of water.

5. **Smoking is taboo!** It makes you sound husky or hoarse, in addition to all the other medical problems it creates of a far more serious nature. Alcohol does not help either. It has a drying effect on the throat and voice and can also contribute to huskiness.

6. **Rest is essential for a healthy voice and body.** If the body is tired the voice will be also. If you have an important speaking engagement, lecture or meeting, find quiet things to do beforehand. Even better, rest as much as possible and talk very little that day.

Enjoy your voice. If you do, others will too.

Further Reading from Kogan Page

Assert Yourself: How To Do a Good Deal Better With Others
A Practical Guide to Effective Listening
Study Skills Strategies: How to Learn More in Less Time
Successful Self-Management: A Sound Approach to Personal Effectiveness

Better Management Skills Series

Effective Meeting Skills
Effective Performance Appraisals
Effective Presentation Skills
The Fifty-Minute Supervisor
How to Communicate Effectively
How to Develop a Positive Attitude
How to Motivate People
Make Every Minute Count
Successful Negotiation
Team Building